BIRDS of PREY

BIRDS of PREY

TOM JACKSON

This pocket edition first published in 2024

First published in a hardback edition in 2021

Copyright © 2024 Amber Books Ltd

Published by
Amber Books Ltd
United House
London N7 9DP
United Kingdom

www.amberbooks.co.uk
Instagram: amberbooksltd
Pinterest: amberbooksltd
Twitter: @amberbooks

ISBN: 978-1-83886-355-5

Project Editor: Anna Brownbridge
Designer: Keren Harragan and Andrew Easton
Picture Research: Terry Forshaw

Printed in China

Contents

Introduction

Nobody is left unimpressed by a bird of prey. The perfect blend of power, elegance and menace, a bird of prey always turns heads. Be they eagles, hawks or falcons, these aerial hunters are used to putting on a show as they hover above a hedgerow or soar and circle overhead before diving in for the kill with devastating speed and accuracy.

Another term for bird of prey is raptor, which refers to the grasping or raptorial feet of these winged killing machines.

The four toes close around prey like a clamp. Each toe is equipped with a talon, or a long, hooked claw – a feature inherited from the bird's dinosaur forebears. The taloned foot is just one item in the raptor's killing kit. All of them have a powerful, hooked beak for ripping and slicing flesh. We

are fortunate that all we have to do is admire these birds. If we had to defend ourselves from them, we would not stand a chance.

ABOVE:
White-bellied sea eagle
The biggest raptors, like this sea eagle, are often fish eaters.

OPPOSITE:
Levant sparrowhawk
Small but perfectly adapted to life as a hunter, this female is pausing for a drink during a long desert migration.

Eagles and Kites

Most birds of prey, around 270 species in total, belong to a family called the Accipitridae. These include hawks, buzzards and some vultures, but the most familiar are eagles. Famed for their impressive size, strength and muscular majesty, eagles are heavy-set birds. They are mostly perch hunters, which means they spend long parts of the day sitting quietly on a vantage point, waiting for the next opportunity to feed. They use their acute senses of hearing and vision to locate a target; then they rise aloft on wings that are both wide and long compared to their overall body length. An eagle generally targets prey on the ground or the surface of water, using its momentum to strike in a fast dive or 'stoop'. The hunter literally lands on its victim, and will often kill with a single hefty blow from its sturdy talons. The Accipitridae does not fall into neat divisions by size. In fact, genetic evidence shows that lineages connect family members of all sizes. The medium-sized members are generally called kites. A typical kite has a weaker and more slender body plan than the eagle does. The hooked bill is considerably less heavy, and the wings are slightly narrower, helping the kite to soar and hover for longer as it scours the ground for prey.

OPPOSITE:
Golden eagle
One of the most widespread raptors, the golden eagle is found across much of the northern hemisphere. With a wingspan of 2m (6.5ft), it is generally the largest hunting bird around.

African hawk-eagle
Small for an eagle, this species lives in the tropical forests of sub-Saharan Africa, although it avoids the thickest rainforests of the Congo Basin. The birds' favoured prey are ground birds, which they flush from hiding before diving in for the kill.

Black eagle
Deceptively tall due to
its slender build, this
big eagle soars above
the forests of Southeast
Asia, India and parts of
tropical China. It is a
specialist nest predator,
plundering the homes
of bats, squirrels and
smaller birds, happily
taking eggs if it can
find them.

OPPOSITE TOP:
Yellow flash
The yellow beak and
cere – the featherless
membrane that covers
the nose bones of raptors
– is the only bright spot
of colour on the black
eagle's body.

OPPOSITE BOTTOM:
Blyth's hawk-eagle
This Southeast Asian
species lives in the drier,
more open forests of
the Malay Peninsula
and Indonesia. The
pale head plumage
indicates that this is a
juvenile; older specimens
have dark heads and
spotted breasts, and the
dark crests grow more
prominent.

Black-and-chestnut eagle

The head of this eagle – a large South American species that preys on monkeys in and around the tallest trees in tropical forests – shows off the eagle eye. As a rule of thumb, eagles can see four to eight times better than a human. Their eyes are the same size as ours, despite their heads being 20 times smaller. The retina has five times the density of light-detecting cells. In simpler terms, an object that comes into clear focus for us at a distance of 1.5m (5ft) will be visible to an eagle 6m (20ft) away.

Booted eagle

This widespread species
is found across much
of the warmer parts
of the Old World. In
winter, the compact
raptor heads to India
and sub-Saharan Africa,
where it is most often
found in dry woodland
areas. In summer, it
passes through desert
regions to circumvent the
Mediterranean and take
up breeding territories
in rocky habitats in
southern Europe
and Central Asia.

OPPOSITE:

Colour forms

The booted eagle is the
smallest eagle species to
enter Europe. There are
two distinct plumage
types seen in the booted
eagle – so named
because its legs and feet
are swathed in feathers.
This is the pale form
with yellow-grey feathers
and a darker head
and wings.

Changeable hawk-eagle

Also known as the crested hawk-eagle, for obvious reasons, this medium-sized eagle is an agile resident of the Indian subcontinent and Southeast Asia. The changeable aspect relates to the way that the birds living in the northern parts of its range show the crest, while that feature is less common in the more hot and humid jungles of the islands in the Indo-Pacific region.

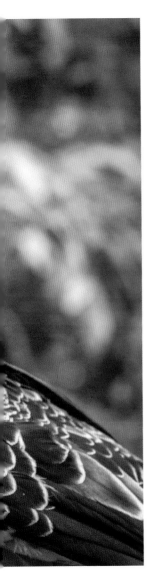

LEFT:
Crowned eagle
An impressive African species that lives in the jungles of the Congo and also drier woodlands to the south. The crowned eagle prefers mammal prey and eats monkeys and small hoofed animals.

BELOW:
Ornate hawk-eagle
Also sometimes called the crested hawk-eagle (like the superficially similar changeable hawk-eagle), this bird lives in the Amazon region and other tropical forests in South and Central America, where it preys mostly on ground birds.

Wing fingers
The tips of this golden eagle's wings have finger-like feathers typical of birds that rely on soaring flight. These reduce drag forces as the wing cuts through fast-moving air, thus performing the same role as the winglets on a modern airliner.

ABOVE:

Territory clash

Golden eagles will defend a feeding territory, as is common among raptors. The territory needs to be big enough to hold a good supply of food, and in cold, boreal parts of its range, the golden eagle will control an area of 200 square km (77 sq miles), among the biggest of any bird of prey. If another eagle glides into this zone, then a fight is inevitable. Combat is largely ritualistic, using aggressive body language to reduce the risk of injury.

Indian spotted eagle
A small eagle that is
resident year round
in the dry forests that
clothe the hills of South
Asia. It is vulnerable to
extinction due to the
threats to these habitats.

RIGHT:
Javan hawk-eagle
An impressive bird with
ruddy, chestnut head
and breast plumage
and a tall crest seen in
both males and females.
The endangered raptor
lives on Java and the
surrounding islands. It
is the national bird of
Indonesia and bears a
resemblance to Garuda,
the bird-like god
of Hindu myth.

Rufous-bellied eagle

A small eagle from the hillside jungles of tropical Asia, this species soars over the treetops and dives between branches to snatch prey out of the air, from tree boughs or the forest floor.

Wedge-tailed eagle
With a wingspan of 2.8m (9ft), this is the largest bird of prey in Australia. It is named after the distinctive diamond profile of the tail when viewed in flight.

LEFT:

Spanish imperial eagle

As the name suggests, this species lives in the southern region of Spain, with an additional population in Portugal.

BELOW:

Steppe eagle

This big booted eagle was once bundled into one species along with the tawny eagle, with which it shares a wintering range in Africa and South Asia. While the tawny eagle stays in those places year round, the steppe eagle migrates to the steppes of Central Asia to breed in summer, before returning to tropical areas in autumn.

Tawny eagle
This is a widespread
species that is found
from the southeastern
fringe of Europe to
southern Africa and from
Mongolia to the south
of India. The eagle likes
dry, forested areas and
grasslands, where it eats
whatever it can lay its
talons on. This one has
picked up some carrion.

OVERLEAF:

Verreaux's eagle
This dark eagle is
found in a patchwork
of populations across
southern Africa, and
can be seen in arid and
broken habitats, such as
cliffs and kopjes
(rock hills).

Brown snake eagle

Widespread across equatorial Africa, this eagle has a specialist diet, as its name suggests. The bird attacks all kinds of snakes, venomous or not. Their legs have a thick skin that fends off the worst of any snake bite, giving time for the eagle to bite off its prey's head and neutralize the threat.

Bateleur

The name of this eagle comes from the French word for 'street performer' or 'tumbler'. The African eagle is an agile flier, even doing loops as it streaks through the air close to the ground, often with its wings in a distinct V-shape.

Red skin

Matching the colour of the face, the legs of the bateleur are covered in a bright red skin. These rugged feet are used to catch pigeons (and smash their eggs) as well as to snatch lizards and small mammals.

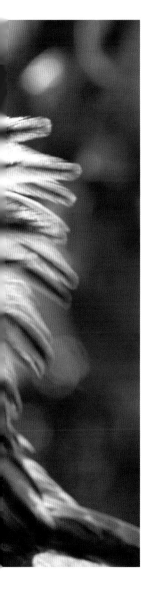

ABOVE:
Short-toed snake eagle
This serpent eagle migrates from the Sahel region
south of the Sahara to southern Europe and the
Middle East. As well as snakes, it preys on lizards and
the occasional small mammal.

LEFT:
Philippine eagle
This species holds the title of the world's biggest eagle
in terms of length (but not weight). The monkey-
eating eagle has a height of 1m (3.3ft) and a wingspan
of 2.2m (7.2ft). The shaggy crest is folded flat against
the head most of the time.

Grey-headed fish eagle

A stocky, fish-eating eagle that lives in India, Sri Lanka and throughout the Malay Peninsula. It is also known as the tank eagle because it is often seen perched near a tank, or a reservoir, as well as natural lakes and rivers. It snatches live fish from the surface or scavenges the banks for dead animals.

OVERLEAF:

Bald eagle

Few raptors are as famous as this North American species. It is the national bird of the United States and it can mostly be seen in the forested mountains. Nevertheless, it is a sea eagle, and survives primarily on a diet of fish plucked from rivers and lakes.

ABOVE:
Feeding perch
As is common with all eagles, the bald eagle rarely
eats on the wing and instead carries its food to a
favourite perch in a tree. The bald eagle hunts for live
prey but will also readily collect dead fish floating on
the surface.

RIGHT:
Bald head
The bald eagle's pale head seen from afar suggests to
many that the big eagle is literally bald. However, the
name is derived from the older term 'balde', which
means 'white', and refers to the bird's sleek white
head plumage.

African fish eagle

In common with all sea eagles, this African fish eagle scavenges for dead fish washed up on the shore (or riverbanks) as well actively hunting for fresher meals. This juvenile eagle, probably less than two years old, is learning that there are other birds that live a similar lifestyle. It is face to face with a marabou stork – also known as the 'undertaker bird' – which appears intent on eating the eagle's fish.

Madagascar fish eagle
Found only along the
northwestern coast of
Madagascar, this is one
of the most endangered
of all raptors. The
destruction of the
island's forest habitats
means there are just a
few hundred of these
impressive birds left.

ABOVE:
Steller's sea eagle
This enormous eagle is built to thrive in the chilly conditions along the Pacific coast of northeastern Asia and the Arctic islands. It flies up river mouths to hunt on salmon heading upstream.

RIGHT:
Cold adaptations
Everything about the Steller's sea eagle is big, helping it to preserve heat. After breeding along the coast of Siberia in summer, in winter the eagles fly south to the coasts of Russia, Japan and Korea.

White-tailed eagle

The white-tailed eagle is a close relative of the bald eagle and lives in a very similar way, albeit in Europe and Asia. Lacking the white head of its American cousin, this species does have the white tail, most visible when seen from above or behind.

RIGHT:
White-bellied sea eagle
This Indo-Pacific bird, which lives along the coasts of India in the west to Australia in the east, looks very distinct from the other sea eagles, with a sleek, pale head and body and dark wings.

OPPOSITE TOP:
Coastal bird
In its Asian range, which includes many islands, the eagle is mostly confined to the coast, while in Australia it comes further inland, following rivers.

OPPOSITE BOTTOM:
Flight feathers
The feathers on the wing and tail overlap to make stiff but lightweight surfaces that can be used to create lift as they cut through the air.

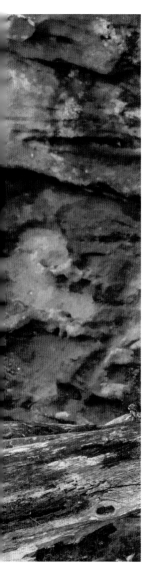

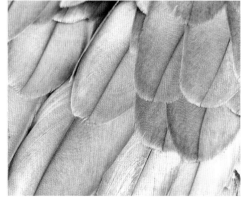

ABOVE:
Black-winged kite
The hooked beak of this medium-sized raptor will tug
and rip this mouse into edible strips. The kite, which
lives in sub-Saharan Africa, India and Southeast Asia,
has an all-encompassing diet, also preying on insects,
frogs and snakes.

RIGHT:
Black-shouldered kite
At first glance, this bird looks the same as its
neighbour pictured left. However, the subtle difference
in wing colouring – the dark patch does not extend
over the whole wing – shows this is a different species
found in Australia.

ABOVE:
Pearl kite
This very small raptor – it is about 20cm (8in) long – lives in the subtropical region of South America, mostly east of the Andes, and outside of the densest jungles. It feeds on lizards and insects.

RIGHT:
White-tailed kite
With a large range stretching from the Pacific Northwest of the United States to Patagonia, this species lives in dry woodlands, shrublands and savannahs. It feeds almost exclusively on rodents.

LEFT:
Black-eared kite
Thought by some authorities to be an eastern
subspecies of the black kite, this bird is so named for
the dark spot behind the eye. It lives in the colder parts
of East Asia and is also found in Europe (alongside
the black kite).

ABOVE:
Winter warmer
In winter, the kite migrates south to warmer regions,
even straying far into the Pacific and appearing
on oceanic islands.

Red kite

The red kite is one of the most common raptors – and most frequently seen – in western Europe. The bird is an able scavenger and so survives well in natural habitats that have been disrupted by human activities. In many parts of its range, however, the red kite is a victim of poisoning from pollutants.

ABOVE:
Plumbeous kite
This South American species is named for it lead-grey plumage. In flight, which is often gliding, red patches can be seen under the wingtips.

LEFT:
Red kite
This kite is easily recognizable from its profile while soaring, with its wings held in a steep V shape. The large, fan-like tail is the reddest part of a decidedly brown bird.

ABOVE:
Whistling kite
This big kite is from New Guinea and New Caledonia. It is named after its distinctive call, which is a descending whistle followed by a series of short, high-pitched rising tones.

RIGHT TOP:
Kite gang
In winter, black kites form flocks and roost together. The collective noun for a kite is a string.

RIGHT BOTTOM:
Black kite
Some ornithologists regard this species as being a complex of subspecies that are found across Eurasia, Africa and Australia. It is resident in tropical areas and migrates north in summer for breeding. The black kite is known to hybridize with red kites.

69

OPPOSITE:

Mississippi kite

Small compared to other kites, this species breeds in North America and migrates to South America in winter. It snatches insects from mid-air and also preys on small vertebrates when it can.

ABOVE:

Snail kite

This highly unusual kite from the wetlands of Central and South America feeds almost exclusively on freshwater apple snails, plucked from waters thick with vegetation.

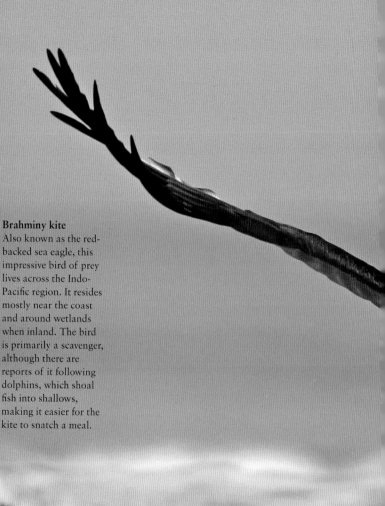

Brahminy kite
Also known as the red-backed sea eagle, this impressive bird of prey lives across the Indo-Pacific region. It resides mostly near the coast and around wetlands when inland. The bird is primarily a scavenger, although there are reports of it following dolphins, which shoal fish into shallows, making it easier for the kite to snatch a meal.

Hawks and Harriers

The smaller members of the Accipitridae family are generally called hawks. More slightly built than their eagle cousins, these birds rely more on agility than strength. A hawk's wings are longer compared to its body length than its heftier relatives, allowing for slower, controlled flight.

Goshawks and sparrowhawks are woodland birds and have longer tails to aid with manoeuvres in confined spaces. The hawks dart out from hidden viewpoints to snatch up prey on or close to thickets of vegetation.

Hawks that live in more open country are generally more robustly built and have a broader, fanned tail. These birds are almost universally known as buzzards in Europe, Africa and Asia; in the Americas, they are still called hawks, and a few disparate related species are even elevated to the level of eagles. That includes the biggest raptor of all, the Philippine eagle. Buzzards specialize in hunting such rodents as squirrels and voles.

Harriers are a subfamily of hawk-like birds that have longer wings and a long, pointed tail. This set-up is ideally suited for quartering, or making low and slow flights that hug the contours of open terrain, such as swamps and moorlands. The harriers prey on small animals lurking in the undergrowth.

OPPOSITE:
Chinese sparrowhawk
The yellow eyes of this hungry hawk tell us that it is a female. The males of this species, generally smaller than the females, as is common in raptors, have red eyes

FAR LEFT TOP:
**Red-thighed
sparrowhawk**
This bird is about the
size of a city pigeon. The
specimen seen here is
the female, which lacks
the ruddy plumage of
the male, from which
the species earns its
name. This small hawk
lives along the edges of
rainforests in West and
Central Africa.

FAR LEFT BOTTOM:
Eurasian sparrowhawk
A widespread bird
that lives year round in
Europe and migrates
from East Africa and
southern Asia into
Siberia each spring to
breed. This is a male,
which is 25 percent
smaller than the female,
which has a wingspan
of up to 80cm (31in). As
the name suggests, this
raptor hunts songbirds.

LEFT:
Bicolored hawk
Living across South
America, this goshawk
prefers lowland habitats
with plenty of cover. It is
a shy species that often
stays out of sight, and
is mostly located by its
'kra-kra' call.

LEFT:

Crested goshawk
The feathery crest
on the back of the
head is generally
flattened, but makes
this Southeast Asian
hunter quite distinctive.
It is adapted to hunt in
thick vegetation and
strikes its prey – mostly
birds, lizards and small
mammals – quickly
before they have the
chance to react.

OVERLEAF LEFT:

Fiji goshawk
This bird of prey is
endemic to the larger
islands in the Fijian
archipelago. It feeds on
other birds, especially
pigeons.

OVERLEAF RIGHT:

Cooper's hawk
This agile woodland
hunter from North
America is also called
the big blue darter or
flying cross, firstly for the
blue markings seen on
the head and secondly
because its long tail gives
it a cruciform shape
when gliding.

RIGHT:

Shikra

In the African part of its range, this bird is called the little banded goshawk and is sometimes treated as a distinct species; the African form, though, is more commonly thought of as a subspecies of the shikra, as it is known in Asia. It lives in a mix of habitats, and small songbirds dive out of trees into thicker foliage as the shikra approaches.

OPPOSITE:

Christmas goshawk

A rare raptor living only on Christmas Island in the Indian Ocean, this is considered a subspecies of the brown goshawk, which is found more widely across the Australian mainland.

OPPOSITE RIGHT:
White-bellied goshawk
This is a striking species found only in New Caledonia, a large island 1200km (750 miles) east of Australia.

LEFT:
Brown goshawk
Widespread throughout the forests and woodlands of Australia, this large hawk also lives in the central parts of Indonesia and New Guinea. It preys on smaller mammals and wetland birds.

RIGHT TOP:

White-eyed buzzard
Although it is not easy to see on this juvenile specimen, the adults of this medium-sized bird have a thick white iris. The species lives in India and there is a second population in mainland Southeast Asia. It soars effortlessly using the finger-like feathers on the tips of its wings to keep it stable in gusty winds and turbulence.

RIGHT BOTTOM:

Grasshopper buzzard
Living in a narrow band of dry grasslands in Africa north of the equator but south of the Sahara Desert, this raptor feeds mainly on insects, as its name suggests.

OPPOSITE:

Grey-faced buzzard
Hunting for lizards, mammals and insects, this buzzard breeds in East Asia in summer and migrates to Southeast Asia for winter.

Common buzzard

As well as being adept at hunting mammals on the ground, the common buzzard will also steal food from other birds. If that is another member of the same species then a fight could break out. A large example of a buzzard, this species is resident year round in Europe; a separate, migratory population winters in southern Africa before flying to eastern Europe and western Siberia.

LEFT:
Grey hawk
This Central American species lives in edge habitats, such as the fringes of forests, riverbanks and coastlines, where one habitat abuts another. It feeds mainly on lizards and snakes.

ABOVE:
Long-legged buzzard
This buzzard is adapted to dry habitats and is resident in North Africa and the Middle East, and migrates to the steppes of Central Asia in summer. It catches burrowing animals, and has been known to stand at the entrance, simply waiting for its next victim to emerge.

LEFT:

Jackal buzzard

An African representative
of the buteonids, or
buzzards, this bird
lives in the south of the
continent. It has a loud
and rather unusual call,
which some confuse with
the barks of the black-
backed jackal – hence the
bird's common name.

ABOVE:

Red-shouldered hawk

A resident of the eastern
part of North America,
this buzzard can be seen
perching on trees or
soaring over woodland
before making plunges
to grab prey. They return
to the treetops to eat,
sometimes building a pile
of food for later.

Forest buzzard

It will come as no surprise that this species lives in evergreen forests, specifically in South Africa and nearby countries. It hunts along the edge of the tree line, preying on a wide range of targets, from ground birds to insects.

Jackal buzzard

Unlike most buzzards, this species is a perch hunter, spending long hours near motionless on a vantage point as it watches and waits for passing prey.

Rough-legged buzzard

One of the few raptors that is found on both sides of the Atlantic – and Pacific. This medium-sized bird of prey spends winter in temperate zones of North America, Europe and Asia, and then migrates to the Arctic in summer to feast on birds that flock there to breed.

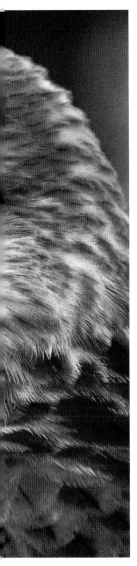

Upland buzzard
This bird is at home in the mountainous regions of Central and East Asia. It moves around from season to season, avoiding areas of deep snow, which make it harder to find prey, which normally consists of small mammals.

RIGHT:

Crested honey buzzard

This is the main Asian species of these unusual raptors. Despite the name, the bird does not eat honey but instead invades bees' nests to get at the tasty maggot-like larvae. The short, scaly feathers around the head are thought to offer protection against stings.

OPPOSITE TOP:

European honey buzzard

The European species actually spends the winter in Africa before migrating as far north as Lapland in summer.

OPPOSITE BOTTOM:

Meat-eater

Although it does occasionally feed on small mammals, in common with its more bloodthirsty cousins, the honey buzzard spends more time digging into wasps' and bees' nests with its feet.

Galapagos hawk
As well as the usual
menu of insects, snakes
and rodents, this raptor
gets the chance to eat
more exotic fare, such
as the hatchlings of
giant tortoises, giant
centipedes and young
marine iguanas. Like a
lot of animals on the
Galapagos Islands in the
Pacific Ocean, this hawk
is fearless of humans.

Zone-tailed hawk
This unusual name
refers to
the black and white
stripes that appear when
the tail is spread into
a fan while the bird is
soaring. This buzzard
lives in Central America
and the tropical parts
of South America.

Harris's hawk

In Latin America, which comprises most of this buzzard's range, the bird is known as a peuco. The extent of the range reaches north into Texas and south to the River Plate. Unlike other raptors, this species is seen hunting in groups and can take out big prey, such as hares and turkeys.

ABOVE:

Black-faced hawk

With its almost comedic
eye mask, this little hawk
lives in the Amazon
rainforest. Very little is
known about what it eats
but it is assumed to be
a perch hunter, making
short glides through
the thick branches
to catch prey.

RIGHT:

Lizard buzzard

Another misnamed
species, this African bird
of prey is more closely
related to the true hawks
than buzzards. They hunt
in grasslands, swooping
down from branches
to grab food from
the ground.

ABOVE:

Eastern chanting goshawk

A resident of the Horn of Africa and the surrounding region, this hawk lives in semi-deserts and grasslands. This one has caught a young sandgrouse. Its chant is a 'whee-pee-pee' call.

RIGHT:

Dark chanting goshawk

Living further west and in less arid habitats than the eastern chanting goshawk, this species has a deeper call with a similar phrasing of 'peeu-peeu-peeu'. This specimen has captured a small snake.

Malagasy harrier
A hunter in the
marshlands of
Madagascar and the
Comoro Islands, this
small bird of prey targets
food by flying low over
the ground. Its main
fare is other birds but
it will supplement that
with rodents and lizards.
As with other marsh
harriers, it builds nests
on the ground.

LEFT:

Western marsh harrier

This is a migratory hunter that divides its time between Africa or India in winter, and Europe or western Asia in summer. The genus name for marsh harriers is *Circus* because they are frequently seen flying in circles as they search for prey on the ground.

ABOVE:

Hen harrier

Named after its penchant for eating wild ground birds – although they do not attack farm animals – this marsh harrier is resident in the temperate parts of Europe and travels north and east to Siberia in summer.

ABOVE:
Sneak attack
About 95 percent of a hen harrier's kills are small mammals. Strange as its sounds, the birds sneak up on targets by approaching low to the ground at an angle that means they stay out of sight until the very last second.

OPPOSITE:
Northern harrier
This is a North American member of the *Circus* genus of marsh harriers. Marsh harriers are some of the few birds of prey species that do not practise monogamy. Instead, one male will mate with several females.

Crane hawk

Classified in its very own genus, this South and Central American bird lives around the edges of forests in tropical lowlands. They have double-jointed ankle bones, which means that the feet are flexible enough to reach into burrows and tree hollows to grab prey of all kinds – bats, squirrels, chicks and snakes.

African harrier-hawk
This atypical raptor from Africa shows off its dexterity by strolling along a rope. In common with the crane hawk of South America, this woodland bird has especially flexible and strong toes, which allow it to climb up trees and suspend from branches or overhanging nests.

OPPOSITE TOP:
Osprey
The osprey is the second
most widely distributed
raptor of all. It is found
in all continents bar
Antarctica, and only the
peregrine falcon lives
in a wider area.

OPPOSITE BOTTOM:
Family of one
The osprey is classified
into its own raptor
family called the
Pandionidae. Some
divide the group into two
species, an eastern and
western osprey.

ABOVE:
Fish hawk
The bird catches fish by
diving into water. It has
flexible toes that swivel
to snatch the slippery
prey, and spikes under
the toes provide
extra grip.

Oily plumage

Once a fish has been secured, the osprey will fly long distances with it to find a safe perch upon which to eat. The bird's feathers are extra oily so they do not become too waterlogged and heavy after their dunking underwater. The osprey can also close its nostrils as it dives into the water to grab prey.

Vultures

Vultures look like they should not belong in a book on birds of prey: they are unloved, ugly and filthy. The birds' long, snaking necks and stooped, leering heads are unsettling, especially when decorated with smears of blood and flecks of flesh. But imagine a world without them – a world where the sky never sees these dark, capable birds gather in tightening circles as they drop down to clear out the dead. Vultures are crucial scavengers, taking a first go at eating whatever scraps they can rip from the remains of deceased animals. Without these avian street cleaners, the world would be a very messy place.

Vultures are a powerful testament to the fact that the basic features of the raptor, namely the adeptly clawed feet and sturdy, hooked beak, can be repurposed from killing fresh prey to ripping up the remains of the already dead. Vultures form two unrelated groups. The Old World vultures of Asia, Africa and Europe are part of the broader Accipitridae family, cosying up with eagles and hawks; the New World vultures found in the Americas make up the Cathartidae. American vultures include condors, which have taken the soaring flight system to its extreme to be the biggest birds of prey of all – although they are not hunters.

OPPOSITE:
Black vulture
One of the most widespread American, or New World, vulture species, this bird is found as far north as New York state and as far south as Uruguay.

Social eaters
Unlike other raptors, vultures are gregarious creatures. These black vultures are roosting in a dead tree in Florida, and in the morning they will search for food as a group. That maximizes the chances that sustenance will be found and makes it easier to defend their food supply from other interested parties.

California condor

This ugly vulture is one of the rarest birds in the world. Its habitat in the dry hills of California and neighbouring states is under extreme pressure from human activity. Thanks to a captive breeding scheme initiated in the 1980s, the number of birds has risen from 22 to nearly 500 today.

RIGHT:

Andean condor

Built to soar up and down the hillsides of the Andes scavenging anything from washed-up whales to the carcasses of vicuñas, this condor has the largest wings by area of any bird. The 3.3m (10.8ft) wingspan allows the bird to soar 160km (100 miles) in just five hours without having to flap its wings once!

OPPOSITE:
Indian vulture
Once a vital part
of the ecosystem
across southern Asia,
this vulture is now
critically endangered.
The main culprit is a
veterinary medicine
called diclofenac, which
persists in livestock after
death. Dead animals
here are traditionally
left for the vultures,
but this chemical has
proven highly toxic. The
population of vultures
has dropped by 95
percent in 20 years. This
is especially problematic
for Zoroastrian
communities in this
region, which expose
their dead in a tower of
silence to be eaten
by vultures.

LEFT:
**Greater yellow-headed
vulture**
This New World vulture
is also called the forest
vulture because it is
mostly found in the
tropical forests of the
Amazon and surrounding
regions. It relies on
bigger vultures living in
this area – namely the
king vulture – to open
up larger carcasses.

RIGHT:

King vulture

This striking bird is well named because it muscles out smaller birds from the prime feeding sites. It is regularly seen following turkey vultures or yellow-headed vultures to carcasses and forcing them to the back of queue as it takes a first go at feeding.

OPPOSITE TOP:

Lesser yellow-headed vulture

While its bulkier namesake is found in forests, this species is most commonly seen on the grasslands of South America, north and south of the great Amazon Basin.

OPPOSITE BOTTOM:

Turkey vulture

Unusually for birds, the turkey vulture, a widespread species found across much of South and Central America as well as the United States, uses its sense of smell to find prey. It flies low over the ground picking up a gas released by decaying bodies.

Frequent tourist

Most vultures are confined to tropical and subtropical areas where there is a good supply of food all year around. The turkey vulture, however, adds to its already extensive range in the Americas by venturing further north than other New World vulture species. In summer, it can be seen beyond the Great Lakes and into southern parts of Canada.

Bearded vulture

This striking Old World species also goes by the names lammergeier and ossifrage. It has a unique way of life that allows it to access the highly nutritious marrow in the centre of bones – something only hyenas and humans are able to do as well. The big bird hauls bones high above rocky outcrops and drops them onto crags so they crack open.

OPPOSITE:

Palm-nut vulture

This African species is very much an outlier in the vulture family in that it uses its beak to break into the husks of palm fruits. More than half of the bird's diet is fruit. The rest is small prey, such as frogs and lizards.

Cape vulture

The main vulture in southern Africa, this big scavenger has a lengthy, flexible neck mostly devoid of long feathers. This anatomical feature allows the bird to reach deep into the carcass of a big animal to get to scraps of meat without becoming too filthy.

Griffon vulture

Also known as the Eurasian griffon, this big vulture is most common in the arid parts of western Asia, although there are small populations in southern Europe. The birds make communal nests on cliffs.

LEFT:
Rüppell's vulture
This African species is known to be a very high flier. In 1973, birds were seen by commercial pilots at an altitude of 11,300m (37,000ft). They can survive in the thin air thanks to special haemoglobin chemicals in the blood that are particularly good at picking up oxygen.

ABOVE:
Cinereous vulture
This big species is the dominant vulture in East Asia. It lives alone or perhaps in pairs, and only gathers in groups where food sources are too big for one bird to defend for itself.

ABOVE:
Lappet-faced vulture
This bird is found in patches across much of Africa
south of the Sahara. It has the same somewhat
unappealing look as the hooded vulture, which lives in
the same area, but the lappet-faced vulture
is considerably larger.

RIGHT:
Hooded vulture
This hooded vulture is feeding on the last few scraps
of sinew on the carcass of a cow in Ethiopia. The
'hood' is a layer of downy feather that runs up the
back of the neck to the top of the head.

White-backed vulture
A white-backed vulture
is having a disagreement
with a black-backed
jackal on the Maasai
Mara grasslands in
Kenya. This part of
the world is famed for
its wealth of wildlife,
so these two expert
scavengers will frequently
come into contact – but
there is food for all.

ABOVE:
White-rumped vulture
This Indian vulture is so named because of the patch
of white feathers on its back.

RIGHT:
Secretary bird
This very unusual raptor sits in its own family called
the Sagittariidae. Although it roosts in treetop nests,
this African bird spends the day hunting on the
ground. It does this by walking through the grass,
flushing out the insects and other prey as it approaches
and jumping on anything within reach.

Falcons and Kestrels

The smallest and nimblest of the birds of prey, falcons form a very distinct family to the other diurnal raptors. The Falconidae has about 60 members living worldwide and this group includes kestrels and caracaras. While superficially similar to hawks, falcons are now known to be a separate lineage, and both groups of hunting birds have converged on the same broad body plan, wing shape and survival strategies. Hooked beaks and grasping, clawed feet are not the preserve of birds of prey, though: the Falconidae are more closely associated with parrots and songbirds, which also exhibit these traits. There are some clear distinctions between falcons and their raptor lookalikes. Falcons are more likely to search for prey while soaring aloft, and many will target other birds in flight as well as look for prey on the ground. While equipped with talons, falcons habitually kill with a bite from their hooked beak. The function of the upper beak's hook is to grip flesh, so the biting falcons have an extra toothlike projection behind this – a tomial – which creates an effective slicing surface. Additionally, the nostril on the beak has a tubercle – a small protuberance. This works to twist and slow the high-speed air entering the nose during a dive. Without the nostril protection, the force of the fast air surging up the nose would damage the bird's lungs.

OPPOSITE:
American kestrel
This dinky bird of prey lives in North and South America. This is the male, which has a bright orange cere at the top of the beak.

ALL PHOTOGRAPHS:
Lanner falcons
The term lanner is said to be derived from a French word for 'coward'. The lanner falcon hunts down bird prey by pursuing them in a horizontal chase. Above, the bird's tomial tooth behind the hook of the beak is clearly visible, as is the tubercle in the nostril.

Prairie falcon

This crow-sized falcon resides in the Great Plains and prairie region of North America between the Rockies and the Mississippi. It closely resembles the peregrine falcon but lives in a very different way to suit its more arid habitat. It preys mainly on small mammals, catching them with a low angle of attack.

Greater kestrel

Also called the white-eyed kestrel, this African bird
of prey lives in the grasslands and semi-deserts of
southern Africa. It is a still hunter, meaning it perches
until it spots prey – mostly insects – and then dives in
for the kill.

Lesser kestrel

Considerably smaller than its greater relative, this
species winters in Africa and then travels to southern
Europe and western Asia in summer to breed. The
female is on the left of the breeding pair shown here.

LEFT:
Eurasian hobby
This bird is a summer
visitor across Europe
and Asia after spending
winter in Africa. The
name is derived from
the Old French for
falcon. Its scientific name
is *Falco subbuteo*, which
refers to how the bird
was originally thought
to be a small version
of a buzzard.

ABOVE:
Gyrfalcon
This is the biggest of
all falcon species, with
females, the larger sex,
being 65cm (26in) tall
with a wingspan of 1.6m
(5.2ft). The birds breed
in the Arctic in summer
before heading south.
A favourite prey
is the ptarmigan.

OPPOSITE TOP:
Amur falcon
Named for the Amur
River, which flows
through eastern Siberia
and northern China,
this small falcon species
spends summer in this
region before migrating
across the Indian Ocean
to southern Africa.

OPPOSITE BOTTOM:
Eleonora's falcon
This falcon breeds on
Mediterranean islands
before heading back to
Madagascar for winter.
The species is named
for Eleanor of Arborea,
the ruler of Sardinia in
the fourteenth century.
She was the first person
to provide protection to
raptors and their nests
in law.

LEFT:
Black-thighed falconet
This is one of the
smallest birds of prey,
at only 15cm (6in) long.
The birds are quite
gregarious – with plenty
of food around, there is
no need for them to live
solitary lives defending a
territory like most birds
of prey.

Peregrine falcon

This is the most widespread raptor of all, living in all continents bar Antarctica. It is a highly specialized hunter of birds – in North America, it is often called a duck hawk. It kills by diving at great speed to gain momentum before flipping at the last second to literally knock the target out of the sky with its feet. This mode of stoop hunting makes the peregrine falcon the fastest animal on the planet, with dive speeds recorded at 389 kph (242 mph).

Red-necked falcon
Present in two separate populations, one in Africa, the other in India, this falcon occupies grassland areas. It usually hunts in breeding pairs, with one bird flying low to flush out putative targets while the second tracks its partner at a greater height ready to dive in for a shared kill.

OPPOSITE:
White-rumped falcon
The white-rumped falcon is limited to the mainland of the Southeast Asian peninsula. This specimen is the female form, which shows off her red upper back and neck.

ABOVE:
Spotted kestrel
The range of this typical kestrel species straddles the
Wallace Line between Sulawesi and New Guinea,
which forms the zoological frontier between the Old
World fauna and the very different animal life of
Australasia and Oceania.

RIGHT:
Madagascar kestrel
Coming to land with its hard-won meal, this kestrel is
one of the few raptors in Madagascar not threatened
by habitat loss.

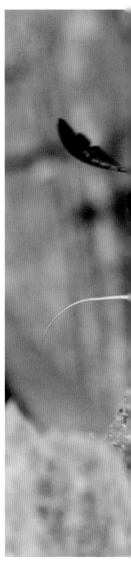

RIGHT:
Merlin
Living across the
northern hemisphere,
the merlin is an expert
bird-hunter. It resides
in woodlands and
among shrubs, using the
vegetation to stay hidden
as it swoops low while
lining up for an attack.

OPPOSITE:
Rock kestrel
Once thought to be
a subspecies of the
Eurasian, or common,
kestrel, this species lives
south of the Congo
Basin, and is most
common in arid habitats.
The bird mostly
eats insects.

Common kestrel
Perhaps better named
the Eurasian kestrel, this
bird lives throughout
Europe, bar the far
north, and some
populations migrate to
India and East Africa in
winter. This male can be
differentiated from the
female by his grey head.

OPPOSITE TOP:
Banded kestrel
This Madagascan species
lives around the coastal
regions of the island
but is missing from the
inland plateau. They are
perch hunters of prey on
the ground.

OPPOSITE BOTTOM:
Bat falcon
Found primarily in
South America as well
as the coast of Central
America, this large
falcon lives in and
around forest clearings.
They perch up high and
swoop in to catch bats,
birds and insects as they
fly across the open space.

RIGHT:

Laughing falcon
Named for its squeaky
and human-like cries,
this forest bird lives in
tropical South America.
It is a hunter of snakes,
pouncing on them in
surprise attacks and
killing with a single bite
to the back of the head.

OPPOSITE TOP:

Cryptic forest falcon
This rather gnomic name
relates to how this falcon
is easily confused with
the other falcon species
that live in tropical South
America. As such, it is
very difficult to spot,
as it hides in plain sight.
It was only identified
in 2003.

OPPOSITE BOTTOM:

Barred forest falcon
More widespread than
its similar relative, the
lined forest falcon, this
bird has wider stripes
on the breast. It lives in
upland forest and hunts
for birds, reptiles and
mammals. It has been
seen to lure birds in by
mimicking their calls.

Crested caracara

Ranging from southern Florida to Tierra del Fuego, this bird is bigger than most other members of the falcon family, second only in size to the gyrfalcon. This specimen is a northern bird. It is an opportunist: it will steal food from vultures and follow cattle (or tractors) to find insects scattered by their hooves, as well as hunt animals – generally small ones.

LEFT:
Black caracara
This caracara lives in the lowland forests of the Amazon and Atlantic coasts. As well as making do with carrion, birds and other live prey, these falcons also wade in clear water, catching fish with their beaks and feet.

ABOVE TOP:
Carunculated caracara
This species only dwells in the highland meadows of the Andes, where it lives as a scavenger. It is a close relative of the mountain caracara.

ABOVE BOTTOM:
Mountain caracara
As the name suggests, this species lives in the dry shrublands of the Andes mountains.

ABOVE:
Striated caracara
This rather eagle-like caracara lives in the extreme south of South America as well as the Falkland Islands. It is primarily a scavenger of dead sheep and seabirds.

RIGHT:
White-throated caracara
Living in the barren grasslands of the Andes and surrounding areas in Chile and Argentina, these big birds do well scavenging among the rubbish left by people.

Beak colour
A crested caracara parent
and child perch in a tree
in Tierra del Fuego. The
younger bird on the right
has a pink and blue beak;
the older one has
an orange beak.

Owls

Is it a bird? Is it a hunter? Yes, but is it a bird of prey? These questions surround the owls, which have several behavioural and anatomical similarities with eagles, hawks and falcons, but also many differences. Owls are specialist nocturnal hunters, something that is very rare among other raptors, and they are grouped separately, in the Strigiformes order, which positions them as second cousins to the eagles and hawks but more distant relations to the falcons and kestrels. Whatever the precise evolutionary history, owls have a very distinct morphology. They are supremely adapted to life in the dark: their eyes are huge and open to the faintest glimmers in the gloom; the feathers along the wing's trailing edge adjust to any turbulence in the air stream, cutting out almost all noise so that an owl's approach is not given away by a single telltale swish or swoosh. The owl's most distinctive feature, however, is its rounded face made from a dish of feathers. This is an acoustic device built to collect sound arriving from in front of the bird and funnel it to the ears. Owl ears, hidden by feathers, are uniquely asymmetric, with one higher on the head than the other. This mismatch allows the owl to locate the sources of any noise with pinpoint accuracy.

OPPOSITE:
Boreal owl
The term 'boreal' means 'northern', and this little owl is found in the conifer forests that circle the northern hemisphere at high latitudes. It is deemed to be a bad omen by local people.

ABOVE:

Northern saw-whet owl

The face of this North American owl glaring from its nest hole belies its small size. This is the smallest owl on that continent, adults being just 20cm (8in) long with a wingspan of 50cm (20in). The 'saw-whet' refers to the harsh sound of the calls.

OPPOSITE:

Togian boobook

Hailing from just three islands off the coast of Sulawesi, Indonesia, this is one of the most recent owl species to be discovered, only formally being described in 2004.

ABOVE TOP:
Feather head
The 'ears' or 'horns' of the long-eared owl are actually feather adornments. Their purpose is to break up the shape of the owl's head so they are harder to spot among the branches.

ABOVE BOTTOM:
Striped owl
Named for the stripes seen on the wings and back, this big species is widespread through Central and South America, although it avoids the rainforests, preferring grasslands and marshes.

Marsh owl
Found in pockets across southern
Africa, this species lives in open
grasslands and wetlands. They nest
and roost on the ground.

PREVIOUS PAGES:
Forward facing
The eyes of an owl, as seen on this short-eared owl, are slightly smaller than that of a human and are less mobile, so the bird turns its whole head to track objects. The eyes also provide a narrower field of vision, only 70 degrees compared to our 140 degrees. Yet this concentrated field of view provides very acute sight and depth perception.

OPPOSITE:
Burrowing owl
This burrowing owl, a small, resourceful species from North and South America, has caught a ring-necked snake to eat. The owl often takes over squirrel burrows to make nests, as do rattlesnakes. When threatened, the owl retreats inside and makes a rattling noise as a defence.

ABOVE:
Spotted owlet
As its name suggests, this is one of the smaller owls, with adults reaching just 20cm (8in) long. It lives in India and mainland Southeast Asia. This one has been photographed mid-blink. As with all birds, owls have three eyelids: one above, another below and a third transparent nictitating membrane that swipes left and right to keep the eye clean.

Little owl

Not all owls are night birds. This species hunts mostly by day, perching up high before swooping in to snatch up any exposed prey, such as this unfortunate vole. At 22cm (8.7in) long and with a wingspan of 56cm (22in), it is one of the smallest owl species in Europe.

Snowy owl

This hefty species lives in the Arctic region. In winter it retreats to the relative shelter of pine forests, but in summer it moves north into the tundra. Given that the Arctic summer has very long day lengths, the snowy owl is mostly a daytime hunter, and so needs its white plumage as camouflage.

ABOVE TOP:
Pel's fishing owl
One of the largest owl species in the world, the adults grow to 60cm (24in) long and have a wingspan of 1.5m (5ft). This African species hunts over calm waters. It swoops low in the dark to snatch fish and frogs.

ABOVE BOTTOM:
Pharaoh eagle-owl
Named after its close association with the Nile Valley, this species is also found in and around the Atlas Mountains in the west of North Africa and throughout the Middle East.

OPPOSITE:
Cape eagle-owl
Located in southern and eastern Africa, this species
prefers rocky and mountainous habitats.

ABOVE:
Great horned owl
Living a similar life to its Eurasian cousin, this
American owl hunts by stealth in dark forests.

LEFT:
Crested owl
A resident of the
Amazon Basin, its pair
of expressive crests are
further elongated by
white stripes that connect
to the beak. This is one
of the dark morphs, with
some birds having paler
plumage.

ABOVE:
Rufous-banded owl
One of the 'earless'
owls, so named because
they have rounded
heads without obvious
protrusions, this species
is a resident of the
equatorial zone of South
America.

OPPOSITE:

Long-whiskered owlet
This tiny owl is found
only in the forest
foothills of the Peruvian
Andes. Very little is
known about its nightly
activities and the species
is classified as vulnerable
to extinction.

ABOVE:

Eurasian pygmy owl
This is the smallest
European owl, with a
length of 19cm (7.5in);
the males are smaller
still. It lives in coniferous
forests and forested
mountain ranges, and
is most common in the
north and east, with its
range extending all the
way to the Pacific.

Pacific screech owl
This medium-sized
bird is confined to
the forests that skirt
the Pacific coast of
Central America.

Eastern screech owl
A screech owl is named
for its unlovely whining
and warbling call. This
species lives in the east of
North America, mostly
in wooded habitats.

Indian scops owl
Scops owls are close
relatives of screech
owls and make similar
cacophonous calls. This
species is the largest of
the scops owls, but is still
barely 25cm (10in) long.
The birds rely on their
colouring to blend into
the bark of branches.

Rufous owl
One of the boobook
owls, this species lives
in tropical forests and
wetlands in northern
Australia and
New Guinea.

LEFT:
Serendib scops owl
Another new species
of owl, only described
in 2004, the Serendib
scops owl lives in Sri
Lanka and was given
endangered status
almost immediately.

BELOW:
**Southern white-faced
owl**
Found south of the
Sahara in grasslands and
dry bush, this species
was once though to be
the same as the northern
white-faced owl, which
lives in forests.

OPPOSITE:

Great grey owl

Snow is no hindrance to the great grey owl. It can hear
the movement of tiny prey under 60cm (24in) of the
stuff and crashes through the fluffy top layer feet first
to grab whatever is down there.

ABOVE:

Tawny owl

The tawny owl is the species that says 'twit twoo'.
Only that is not really true. Firstly, the owl says just
'twit' – which is actually 'ke-wick'. Then a nearby
male with territorial rights to defend will reply with
a 'twoo', which is more accurately 'hoo-hoo-oooo'.

ABOVE:
Red owl
The red owl is a rare
and endangered species
from Madagascar under
increasing threat from
habitat destruction.

RIGHT:
Barn owl
The barn owl is the
most widespread of all
owl species. It lives on
all continents barring
Antarctica and is found
in all habitats south of
the cold forests. Unlike
most other owls, which
are perch hunters,
the barn owl traverses
the ground for prey.

In the Nest

The day-to-day activity of a raptor lends itself to a solitary life. There is no room for sharing when survival demands each bird scours the landscape for prey and must strike first time with no warning to secure each meal. Most raptors will defend a large territory and patrol it alone. However, this belies the fact that these big hunting birds maintain strong bonds with mates, generally pairing for life.

A male raptor is invariably smaller than the female, and he woos her with acrobatic flight displays and gifts of sticks and other nest-building equipment. Part of the courtship or later re-enforcing play involves the couple handing off twigs from one to the other like an aerial relay team. Sometimes they stay locked in a clawed grip and swirl through the sky.

The female builds the nest, which is often located in a high place and has an elaborate construction. It's the mate's job to collect the required materials and keep his partner supplied with food as she broods the eggs. Big birds stick at one or two eggs, while smaller raptors might lay six. After hatching, the male will provide food for the nestlings, too. The female might team up with him to flush out larger prey, such as rabbits or ground birds, but her focus is protecting the helpless chicks.

OPPOSITE:
Steppe eagle chick
A pair of chicks, or eaglets, wait for their next meal. While their mother guards the nest, their father will soon return with a meaty tidbit.

Home sweet home
Bald eagles have enormous nests, often near 2m (6.5ft) wide. This is not only because the birds require a big, safe platform: good nesting sites are reused year on year. Over generations, nests grow very large. The biggest ever seen was in Florida and was 2.5m (8ft) wide and 6m (20ft) deep!

LEFT:

Black kite chicks

These widespread birds breed at different times of the year. In South Asia, the eggs are laid in winter so the chicks fledge before the monsoon; in Europe, breeding takes place in summer.

ABOVE:

Hen harrier chicks

These birds hatched from eggs laid in a simple nest made on the ground. The chicks will be fully fledged at the age of 36 days, but will not by fully mature until the age of two.

Helping out
These New Zealand falcon chicks are fed strings
of meat by their mother. They are still too immature
to tear off their own mouthfuls. When very young,
they were fed predigested, regurgitated food.

RIGHT:
Grub's up
A common kestrel serves up dinner for her three chicks
inside a nesting box. The male will have handed his
mate the mouse meal before setting off to find more
food. The female will rip small strips of flesh and feed
the chicks in turn.

RIGHT TOP:

New home

A male bat falcon hands over a dead bat to his mate. The pair of falcons from South America did not dig out this neat nest. Instead they refurbished a hole left by a parrot or woodpecker.

RIGHT BOTTOM:

Rock ledge

A female peregrine falcon prepares to protect her precious eggs, which are high on a cliff. These fast birds pair for life.

OPPOSITE TOP:

Fluffy camouflage

These Eurasian eagle owlets emerge from the eggs with a fluffy grey down that helps them to blend in with their sandy nest.

OPPOSITE BOTTOM:

Moving on

These northern saw-whet owlets have been abandoned by their mother. Only the father is left to supply them with food. However, this is completely normal. Each season, a female will have time to produce two broods, each one with a different mate.

Hairy nest
Lappet-faced vultures build their big nests from sticks and leaves, and line them with hair and skin from dead animals. This pair will brood one or two eggs and their big chicks will take nearly five months to fledge.

ABOVE:
Crested caracara nest
These big birds build
wide nests in trees.
They lay eggs in spring
and early summer,
which in their southern
homeland is October
and November.

RIGHT:
Fish supper
An osprey chick gets
a much needed scrap
of fish. These birds build
nests high above a
stretch of water, which
serves as a suitable
hunting ground.

Rising above

Ferruginous hawks build their nests raised above the surrounding area. That could be in a tree, atop a pile of rocks or on an artificial platform provided by people to boost the hawk population, as here in Idaho.

Picture Credits

Alamy: 7 (Danny Laredo), 10/11 (Blickwinkel), 16 (Buiten-Beeld), 24 (KD Leperi), 26/27 (Minden Pictures), 28/29 (Brad Leue), 50/51 & 58 (Biosphoto), 62 (Blickwinkel), 63 (Tierfotoagentur), 64/65 (Waterframe), 66 (Victor Harris), 74 (Nature Picture Library), 80 (Greg Vaughn), 83 (FLPA), 94 (RooM The Agency), 99 bottom (Arterra Picture Library), 104 (Agami Photo Agency), 114/115 (Panoramic Images), 118 bottom (Alan Tunnicliffe), 122 (Max Allen), 142/143 (Minden Pictures), 149 top (Riccardo Sala), 158/159 (Anna Stowe), 163 (Blickwinkel), 169 bottom (Minden Pictures), 175 (Simon Stirrup), 181 (Agami Photo Agency), 182 top (All Canada Photos), 182 bottom (Andrew Bartlett), 183 (AfriPics.com), 186 (Brian Parker), 190 (Media Drum World), 194 (Nature Picture Library), 195 (All Canada Photos), 200 (Dhaval Shah), 207 (Rolf Nussbaumer Photography), 212 (Anil Sharma), 213 (Richard Clarkson), 214 (Juniors Bildarchiv), 215 (Rolf Nussbaumer Photography), 218/219 (Nature Picture Library), 220 (All Canada Photos)

Dreamstime: 13 top (Ecophoto), 25 (Dikkyoesin), 32/33 (Ndp), 34/35 (Anton Opperman), 36 (Amreshm), 41 (Dennis Jacobsen), 44/45 (Lawrence Weslowski Jr), 46 (Brian Kushner), 72/73 (Volodymyr Kucherenko), 77 (Rafael Cerqueira), 82 (Amreshm), 86 top (Amreshm), 86 bottom (Dennis Jacobsen), 90 (Nsirlin), 92 (Ecophoto), 95 top (Abraham Badenhorst), 95 bottom (Wildlife World), 96/97 (Liqiang Wang), 99 top (Slowmotiongli), 100 (Ndp), 102/103 (Rudolf Ernst), 106 & 107 (Simon Fletcher), 110 (StockPhotoAstur), 111 (Mycteria), 113 (Brian Kushner), 116/117 (Ian Dyball), 119 (Wang LiQiang), 120/121 (Adventuring Dave), 123/124 (Steve Byland), 126 top (Michael Elliott), 126 bottom (Kojihirano), 127 (Pixattitude), 128 (EPhotocorp), 129 (Dmitrii Kashporov), 130 (Nick Biemans), 131 bottom (Musat Christian), 132/133 (Thomas Lozinski), 134 (Mikelane45), 135 (Suzanne Schoepe), 137 top (Hedrus), 137 bottom (Lukas Blazek), 138 (Jacek Placek), 139 (Wildlife World), 140 (Ecophoto), 141 (Caglar Gungor), 145 (Mogens Trolle), 148 (Christokruger), 149 bottom (Neal Cooper), 150/151 (Donald Fink), 153 (Martin Mecnarowski), 156 top (Jirapath09), 157 (Thawats), 160 (Ecophoto), 162 (Wayan Sumatika), 164 (Scott Ward), 165 (Duncan Noakes), 170/171 (Gueret Pascale), 172 (SWF1), 173 bottom (Frank Cornelissen), 174 (Dalia Kvedaraite), 178 (Martin Kubik), 180 (Lynn Bystrom), 184/185 (Mycteria), 187 (Assoonas), 188/189 (Juan Pablo Fuentes Serrano), 192 (Stu Porter), 193 (Brian Kushner), 199 (Jill Lang), 202 (Sharon Jones), 221 (Brian Kushner), 222/223 (Fischer 0182)

Dreamstime/Agami Photo Agency: 76 top, 84, 85, 108/109, 168, 196

Dreamstime/Ondrej Prosicky: 101, 105, 136, 146, 173 top, 205

FLPA: 203 bottom (Minden Pictures/Martin Willis), 206 (Biosphoto/Dominique Halleux)

Getty Images: 12 (Digital Vision), 60 (Juan Carlos Vindas), 71 (Michael J Cohen), 191 top (Digital Vision)

iStock: 210/211 (BirdImages)

Shutterstock: 6 (Wang LiQiang), 8 (Michal Winger), 13 bottom (Itsuky), 14/15 (Christopher Becerra), 17 (Jesus Giraldo Gutierrez), 18/19 (amrishw), 20 (Jordan Confino), 21 (Joanne Weston), 23 & 23 (Vladimir Kogun Michael), 30 (Jesus Giraldo Gutierrez), 31 (Ondrej Prosicky), 37 (Albert Beukhaf), 38/39 (Clayton Harrison), 40 (Michal Lukaszewicz), 42/43 (HelloRFZcool), 47 (cvrestan), 48/49 (Mark Sheridan-Johnson), 52 (Vladimir Soltys), 53 (Sergey Uryadnikov), 54/55 (Vaclav Sebek), 56 (Anne Powell), 57 top (Thanakorn Hongphan), 57 bottom (Leisuretime70), 59 (Jeff Grabert), 61 (Phoo Chan), 67 (Rafael Goes), 68 (Terry Dell), 69 top (Ondrej Prosicky), 69 bottom (Vladimir Kogan Michael), 70 (Dan Rieck), 76 bottom (Karel Bartik), 78/79 (Kurit Afshen), 81 (Michael Schober), 87 (Richard Cook), 88/89 (Veselin Gramatikov), 91 (Alitellioglu), 93 (Dan Rieck), 98 (Martine Liu 58), 112 (Ranchorunner), 118 top (Wang LiQiang), 131 top (Bildagentur Zoonar), 144 (Ishor Gurung), 152 (Txanbelin), 154 (Ajith Everester), 155 (Rosemarie Kappler), 156 bottom (Rolando Criniti), 161 (Butterfly Hunter), 166 (Wayne Tuckwell), 167 top (Agami Photo Agency), 167 bottom (Chelsea Sampson), 169 top (Pedro Bernardo), 176/177 (Nick Pecker), 191 (Michal Ninger), 197 (Krasula), 198 (Matt Elliott), 203 top (Sasika Peiris), 204 (Adamikarl), 208 (Vladimirs Suscinskis), 216 top (Chelsea Sampson), 216 bottom (Ken Griffiths), 217 top (WildMedia), 217 bottom (Ivan Deng)